Beca
Wine Can't
Solve
Everything

30 Journal Prompts for Healing and Letting Go

By Leah C. Carlson

Wine Can't Solve Everything:
30 Daily Prompts for Healing and Letting Go

Edited by Regan R. Richardson

Published in the United States of America by
Story Haven Press

First paperback edition 2025.

ISBN 979-8-9896249-3-5 Paperback

Dedication

For Sarah
who was there for me.

Welcome...

to your 30-day journey of self-discovery, healing, and empowerment. This journal has been thoughtfully crafted for anyone who has experienced divorce or a break-up by providing a supportive space for you to reflect, grow, and embrace new beginnings.

Divorce is one of life's most challenging transitions, often leaving us with a mix of emotions and a sense of uncertainty about the future. However, it also presents an opportunity to reconnect with yourself, redefine your goals, and rediscover your inner strength. This journal aims to guide you through this process with daily writing prompts designed to inspire, uplift, and encourage personal growth.

Each day, you will find a new prompt that invites you to explore different aspects of your journey. From reflecting on past experiences to envisioning a bright future, these prompts will help you navigate your emotions, set healthy boundaries, and celebrate your resilience.

Remember, there is no right or wrong way to approach these prompts. Write from your heart, be honest, and allow your thoughts to flow freely. This journal is your private sanctuary where you can express your true self without judgment.

As you embark on this 30-day journey, be kind to yourself. Healing is not a linear process, and it's okay to have ups and downs. Celebrate your progress, no matter how small, and give yourself the grace to move at your own pace.

You are stronger than you know, and this journal will remind you of that strength every step of the way. Embrace this time as a period of renewal and transformation. Your best days are ahead. This is the beginning of a beautiful new chapter in your life.

With love and encouragement,

Leah

Introduce yourself.
Write about who
you are beyond
your marital status.

What are your
passions,
strengths, and
dreams?

What does a
fresh start
look like to you?

Describe your ideal
new beginning
without any
thoughts on how
you will make
it happen.

Just dream.

Reflect on a time when you felt particularly strong or resilient.

How can you draw on that strength now?

Healing takes time.

How can you practice patience with yourself during this process?

Share a vulnerable moment or feeling you've experienced during your divorce.

Would it help to share this with someone you trust?

What steps can you take today to cultivate inner peace amidst the chaos you are going through mentally, emotionally, and physically?

Write about the boundaries you need to set in your life to protect your well-being.

This includes from family, friends, social media, co-workers, etc.

What would you tell your in-laws if you never had to see them again?

Have fun with this.

What do you
need to let go of to
move forward?

Who are the top people in your support system and what do you need from them during this time?

Pick one person to contact and call them.

What is one thing about your ex that you are glad you never have to deal with again?

Feel free to make a whole list.

What is something you are excited about now that you can priroritize your own needs?

What's a hobby
or passion you used
to do, but stopped
having time for?

Pick a day to start
it again.

Write about your financial goals.

How does your budget need to change?

What's a change you resisted in the past, but it worked out in the end?

Make a list of things about yourself that are unique and irreplaceable.

What was the last challenge you overcame before your divorce?

Can you use anything you learned during that challenge to help you now?

One year from today, when you wake up, what do you want your day to look like?

Today's Date ______

What do you now
think love is?

What do you
think love is not?

Being creative is
healing.

What creative thing
can start today that
you can do on
a regular basis for
the next six months?

What beliefs or thoughts about divorce do you need to let go of now that you are the one getting divorced?

Name three things you are grateful for at this very moment.

What have you learned about yourself that surprised you during this process?

What does self care look like for you?

What emotions are you feeling today?

What can you do to manage them so they don't feel so overwhelming?

Forgiveness
is letting go of the
outcome you
expected.

What does
forgiveness
mean to you?

What is one win you've achieved since going through the divorce process?

On the days you
do not feel like getting
out of bed, what forced
you to finally do it?

It’s fine if you don’t…
sometimes.

Write yourself a letter, as though you are writing it to a friend who is going through a divorce.

How would you encourage them?

YOU MADE IT!

Reflect on the
last thirty prompts.

What have you
learned
about yourself?

Bonus:

Do you have a favorite prompt?

If so, what did you like about it?

About The Author

Leah Carlson is completing an M.A in Creative Writing at the University of Denver. She is writing a memoir about doing AncestryDNA as an adoptee and her surprising result.

www.leahccarlson.com
Instagram: @newchapterchic
Facebook.com/newchapterchic
TikTok: @newchapterchic

Made in the USA
Columbia, SC
20 May 2025

58176366R20041